Entenmann's ®

BAKE SHOP

PaRragon

Bath · New York · Singapore · Hong Kong · Cologne · Delhi
Melbourne · Amsterdam · Johannesburg · Auckland · Shenzhen

This edition published in 2013
Copyright © Parragon Books Ltd
Chartist House
15-17 Trim Street
Bath, BA1 1HA, UK
www.parragon.com

Copyright © Parragon Books Ltd 2013

Internal design: Sabine Vonderstein, Köln
Photography: Jo Kirchherr
Food: Matthias Ludwigs
Prop styling: Sabine Vonderstein

ISBN: 978-1-4723-2722-2
Printed in China

Notes for the reader:
All spoon measurements are level.
Unless otherwise stated milk is assumed to be whole and eggs are
medium-size.
Preparation and cooking times may vary due to personal cooking techniques
& type of oven being used.
WARNING FOR NUT ALLERGIES: Please be aware that some of the ready prepared
ingredients used in the recipes may contain nuts, always check prepackaged ingredients
before use.
Recipes using raw or very lightly cooked eggs should be avoided by
infants, the elderly, pregnant women, and anyone with a chronic condition.

CONTENTS

Blueberry
MUFFIN SUPREME

Makes 12 muffins

Muffin Batter

3 cups all-purpose flour
¾ teaspoon salt
1 tablespoon baking powder
½ teaspoon baking soda
1 cup sugar
8 tablespoons (1 stick) butter, softened
Finely grated zest from one lemon
2 tablespoons vegetable oil
2 large eggs
1 cup sour cream
½ cup whole milk
½ teaspoon lemon extract, optional
2 cups fresh blueberries

- Preheat oven to 375°F.

- Grease a 12-cup muffin pan or line with 12 paper baking cups.

- Sift together the flour, salt, baking powder and baking soda into a bowl. Set aside.

- In a large mixing bowl, beat the sugar, butter, lemon zest and vegetable oil until light and creamy. Beat in the eggs one at a time. Whisk in the sour cream, milk and lemon extract.

- Add half the flour mixture and stir until combined. Fold in the rest of the flour and mix thoroughly.

- Fold in the blueberries with a spatula until just combined.

- Fill each cup with batter and bake for 25–30 minutes until golden brown.

- When cool, remove muffins from the cups and serve.

Our founder, William Entenmann, was a baker from Stuttgart, Germany, who learned his trade from his father. William's first job in America was in a bread bakery.

Jelly Donut MUFFINS

Makes 12 muffins

Muffin Batter

2   cups all-purpose flour
1   tablespoon baking powder
Pinch of salt
½   cup sugar
2   large eggs
1   cup whole milk
6   tablespoons vegetable oil
1   teaspoon vanilla extract
¼   cup strawberry
     or raspberry jelly

Topping

8   tablespoons (1 stick) butter
¾   cup sugar

- Preheat the oven to 400°F.

- Grease a 12-cup muffin pan or line with 12 paper baking cups.

- Sift together the flour, baking powder and salt into a large bowl. Stir in the sugar.

- Lightly beat the eggs in a large bowl, then beat in the milk, oil and vanilla extract. Make a well in the center of the dry ingredients and pour in the beaten liquid ingredients. Stir gently until combined.

- Spoon half the batter into the muffin cups. Add a teaspoon of jelly to the center of each, then spoon in the remaining batter.

- Bake in the preheated oven for about 20 minutes, until well risen, golden brown and firm to the touch.

- To make the topping, melt the butter. Spread the sugar in a wide, shallow bowl. When the muffins are baked, let them cool for 5 minutes. Dip the tops of the muffins in the melted butter, then roll in the sugar.

- Serve warm or transfer to a wire rack and let cool completely.

Carrot Cake
MUFFINS

Makes 12 muffins

Muffin Batter

2 cups all-purpose flour
1 tablespoon baking powder
Pinch of salt
1 teaspoon apple pie spice
½ cup firmly packed light
   brown sugar
1 cup grated carrots
½ cup chopped walnuts
   or pecans
½ cup golden raisins
2 large eggs
¾ cup whole milk
6 tablespoons vegetable oil
Finely grated zest and juice
   of 1 orange
Strips of orange zest, to decorate

Frosting

½ cup soft cream cheese
3 tablespoons butter, softened
⅓ cup confectioners' sugar

- Preheat the oven to 400°F.

- Grease a 12-cup muffin pan or line with 12 paper baking cups.

- Sift together the flour, baking powder, salt and apple pie spice into a large bowl. Stir in the sugar, grated carrots, walnuts and golden raisins.

- Lightly beat the eggs in a large bowl, then beat in the milk, oil, grated orange zest and orange juice. Make a well in the center of the dry ingredients, and pour in the beaten liquid ingredients. Stir gently until just combined; do not overmix.

- Spoon the batter into the muffin pan. Bake in the preheated oven for about 20 minutes, until well risen, golden brown and firm to the touch.

- Let the muffins cool for 5 minutes, then transfer to a wire rack and let cool completely.

- To make the frosting, put the cream cheese and butter in a bowl, and sift in the confectioners' sugar. Beat together until light and fluffy. When the muffins are cold, spread the frosting on top of each, then decorate with strips of orange zest. Chill the muffins in the refrigerator until ready to serve.

Double Chocolate Chip MUFFINS

Makes 8 muffins

Muffin Batter

8   tablespoons (1 stick) butter, softened
½   cup sugar
2   large eggs
¾   cup self-rising flour
½   cup semisweet chocolate chips
½   cup cocoa powder

- Preheat the oven to 375°F.
- Grease an 8-cup muffin pan or line with 8 paper baking cups.
- In a bowl, sift together the flour and cocoa powder. Set aside.
- In a large mixing bowl, beat together the butter, sugar and eggs until smooth.
- Add half the dry ingredients and stir until combined. Add the remaining dry ingredients. Fold in the chocolate chips until combined.
- Spoon the batter into the prepared muffin cups.
- Bake in the preheated oven for 20–25 minutes or until well risen and springy to the touch.
- Transfer to a wire rack and leave to cool.

In 1898, William opened his own bakery in Brooklyn, New York. He delivered fresh-baked goods door-to-door in a horse-drawn wagon.

Lemon Poppy Seed MUFFINS

Makes 12 muffins

Muffin Batter

2 cups all-purpose flour
½ teaspoon salt
1½ teaspoons baking powder
¼ teaspoon baking soda
8 tablespoons (1 stick) unsalted butter, softened
1 cup sugar
Finely grated zest from 2 lemons
2 large eggs
2 tablespoons lemon juice
1 cup sour cream
2 tablespoons poppy seeds

Glaze

1 tablespoon lemon juice
3 tablespoons confectioners' sugar

- Preheat oven to 350°F.

- Grease a 12-cup muffin pan or line with 12 paper baking cups.

- Whisk together the flour, salt, baking powder and baking soda in a bowl, and set aside.

- In a mixing bowl, beat the butter, sugar and lemon zest until light and creamy. Beat in the eggs one at a time, mixing thoroughly. Stir in a third of the flour mixture until just combined. Stir in the lemon juice and half of the sour cream until combined.

- Fold in half of the remaining flour mixture, and stir until combined. Stir in the remaining sour cream, flour and poppy seeds.

- Fill the cups with batter. Bake for 20-25 minutes or until golden brown and a toothpick inserted in the center comes out clean. While the muffins are baking, make the glaze. Mix the lemon juice and confectioners' sugar together to form a thin glaze.

- Remove the muffins from the oven and cool for 5 minutes. Brush the lemon glaze evenly over the top of each muffin, when cool enough to handle.

Frosted Cream Cheese MUFFINS

Makes 12 muffins

Muffin Batter

½ cup soft cream cheese
1 tablespoon confectioners' sugar
2 cups all-purpose flour
1 tablespoon baking powder
Pinch of salt
½ cup firmly packed light brown sugar
½ cup sugar
2 large eggs
1 cup sour cream
6 tablespoons vegetable oil
Finely grated zest of 1 lemon
2 teaspoons fresh lemon juice

Frosting

½ cup soft cream cheese
⅓ cup confectioners' sugar
2 teaspoons fresh lemon juice

- Preheat the oven to 400°F.

- Grease a 12-cup muffin pan or line with 12 paper baking cups.

- Put ½ cup of the cream cheese in a bowl. Sift in 1 tablespoon of the confectioners' sugar and beat together.

- Sift together the flour, baking powder and salt into a large bowl. Stir in the brown and white sugar.

- Lightly beat the eggs in a large bowl, then beat in the sour cream, oil, lemon zest and lemon juice. Make a well in the center of the dry ingredients and pour in the liquid ingredients. Stir gently until combined; do not over mix.

- Spoon half the batter into the muffin cups. Add a spoonful of the cream cheese mixture to the center of each, spoon in the remaining batter. Bake in the preheated oven for about 20 minutes, until well risen, golden brown and firm to the touch. Let the muffins cool for 5 minutes, then transfer to a wire rack, and let cool completely.

- To make the frosting, put the cream cheese in a bowl and sift in the confectioners' sugar. Add the lemon juice, and beat well together. Spread the frosting on top of the muffins. Chill in the refrigerator until ready to serve.

Vanilla Sugar
COOKIES

Makes about 12 cookies

Dough

1½ cups all-purpose flour

12 tablespoons (1½ sticks) cold
    butter, cut into pieces

1 cup sugar

1 teaspoon vanilla extract

Sugar or cocoa powder, for dusting

- Preheat the oven to 350°F.

- Grease several baking sheets.

- Sift the flour into a large bowl. Add the butter, and rub it in with your fingertips until the mixture resembles fine breadcrumbs. Stir in the sugar and vanilla extract, and mix together to form a firm dough.

- Roll out the dough on a lightly floured counter to a thickness of ½ inch. Stamp out 12 hearts with a heart-shaped cookie cutter. Arrange the hearts on the prepared baking sheet.

- Bake in the preheated oven for 15–20 minutes, or until just colored. Transfer to a wire rack and let cool completely.

- Dust with a little sugar or cocoa powder just before serving.

When William's son was taken ill, the family moved to Bay Shore, Long Island, at the doctor's suggestion and opened a bakery on Main Street. Later, William Jr. took the reins of the bakery, including 30 home-delivery routes.

Chocolate Chip COOKIES

Makes about 30 cookies

Dough

2¼ cups all-purpose flour
1   teaspoon baking soda
1   teaspoon salt
2   sticks butter, softened
¾   cup firmly packed light
     brown sugar
¾   cup sugar
1   teaspoon vanilla extract
2   large eggs
2   cups semisweet chocolate chips
1   cup chopped walnuts (optional)

- Preheat oven to 375°F.

- Line several baking sheets with parchment paper.

- Add the flour, baking soda and salt to a small mixing bowl and mix together. Set aside.

- In another bowl, beat the butter, brown sugar, white sugar and vanilla extract until light and fluffy.

- Add the eggs one at a time, beating thoroughly after each addition. Stir in the flour mixture until combined. Stir in the chocolate chips and nuts (optional). Mix the dough well.

- Drop the cookie dough by rounded tablespoons on prepared baking sheets about 3 inches apart.

- Bake for about 10 minutes or until lightly browned around the edges.

- Let sit on the baking sheets for 2 minutes, and then move to wire cooling racks to cool completely.

White Chocolate
COOKIES

Makes about 30 cookies

Dough

8   tablespoons (1 stick) butter, softened

½   cup firmly packed light brown sugar

1   egg, lightly beaten

1¾ cups self-rising flour

Pinch of salt

¾   cup white chocolate pieces

⅓   cup chopped Brazil nuts

- Preheat the oven to 375°F.

- Grease several baking sheets.

- Place the butter and sugar in a large bowl, and beat together until light and fluffy. Gradually add the egg, beating well.

- Sift the flour and salt into the creamed mixture, and blend well. Stir in the white chocolate chunks and chopped nuts.

- Place teaspoonfuls of the batter on the baking sheets, putting no more than 6 on each sheet because the cookies will spread during cooking.

- Bake in the preheated oven for 10–12 minutes or until just golden brown.

- Transfer the cookies to wire racks to cool completely.

Peanut Butter COOKIES

Makes about 26 cookies

Dough

8 tablespoons (1 stick) butter, softened

½ cup crunchy peanut butter

½ cup sugar

½ cup firmly packed light brown sugar

1 egg, beaten

½ teaspoon vanilla extract

⅔ cup all-purpose flour

½ teaspoon baking soda

½ teaspoon baking powder

Pinch of salt

1½ cups rolled oats

- Preheat the oven to 350°F.

- Grease several baking sheets.

- Place the butter and peanut butter in a bowl, and beat together. Beat in the sugar and brown sugar, then gradually beat in the egg and vanilla extract.

- Sift the flour, baking soda, baking powder and salt into the bowl and stir in the oats.

- Place spoonfuls of the cookie dough onto the baking sheets, spaced well apart to allow for spreading. Flatten slightly with a fork.

- Bake in the preheated oven for 12 minutes or until lightly browned.

- Let cool on the baking sheets for 2 minutes, then transfer to wire racks to cool completely.

Midnight COOKIES

Makes about 25 cookies

Dough

8 tablespoons (1 stick) butter, softened
1 cup sugar
1 egg, lightly beaten
½ teaspoon vanilla extract
1 cup all-purpose flour
⅓ cup unsweetened cocoa
½ teaspoon baking soda

- Preheat the oven to 350°F.

- Line several baking sheets with parchment paper.

- Place the butter and sugar in a large bowl and beat together until light and fluffy. Add the egg and vanilla extract and mix until smooth. Sift in the flour, cocoa and baking soda and beat until well mixed.

- With dampened hands, roll walnut-size pieces of the dough into smooth balls. Place on the baking sheets, spaced well apart.

- Bake in the preheated oven for 10–12 minutes or until set.

- Let cool on the baking sheets for 5 minutes, then transfer the cookies to wire racks to cool completely.

Entenmann's prospered through the early part of the 20th century. The legend tells us that our baked goods were enjoyed by many prominent families such as the Morgans and the Vanderbilts.

Simple DONUTS

Makes 10–12 donuts

Batter

1   cup whole milk

4   packages (9 teaspoons) active
     dry yeast

2   cups all-purpose flour

2   tablespoons sugar

½   teaspoon salt

3   egg yolks

1   teaspoon vanilla extract

4   tablespoons butter, softened

Vegetable oil for greasing baking
     sheet and frying

• Heat the milk until lukewarm, and dissolve the yeast into the milk. Add 1½ cups of the flour into the mixture, and set aside for 30 minutes.

• In a stand mixer fitted with a paddle attachment, add the sugar, salt, egg yolks and vanilla and mix on low until smooth. Add the butter and milk and flour mixture from step 1 and mix slowly. Change the paddle attachment to a dough hook and add the remaining flour. Mix slowly until the dough is smooth. Refrigerate the mixture for 60 minutes.

• Roll the dough onto a floured surface. The dough should be about ½-inch thick. Using a donut cutter, cut out the donuts. Place on a greased baking sheet, cover with plastic wrap and leave in a warm place. The donuts should rise to nearly double the original size and spring back when touched.

• Heat 3 inches of vegetable oil in a heavy bottomed pan. The oil should be 360°F in temperature.

• Carefully place the donuts one at a time into the hot oil. Fry for 2 minutes on each side or until golden brown. Remove with a slotted spoon and drain on a wire rack.

Sour Cream DONUTS

Makes 24 donuts

Batter

1   cup sugar
3   eggs
1   cup sour cream
1   teaspoon vanilla extract
3½ cups all-purpose flour
1   teaspoon baking soda
1   teaspoon baking powder
½   teaspoon salt
¼   teaspoon nutmeg
Vegetable oil for frying

Glaze (optional)

1½ cups confectioners' sugar
3–4 tablespoons water
    (or whole milk)

- In a large bowl, beat sugar and eggs thoroughly. Add the sour cream and vanilla extract. Mix well.

- Add the dry ingredients and mix well again. Turn onto floured board and knead for 5 minutes. The dough should be fairly soft.

- Roll out the dough to ¼-inch thickness. Cut with a floured donut cutter.

- In a saucepan, heat 3 inches of vegetable oil to 360°F. Cook the donuts in batches by dropping into the hot oil. Fry for 2 minutes on both sides or until golden brown.

- Remove with a slotted spoon and drain on a paper towel or wire rack.

- To make the glaze, place the sugar in a bowl, and slowly mix in the water or milk until smooth.

- Pour the glaze over the cooled donuts.

Jelly
DONUTS

Makes 10 donuts

Batter

Vegetable oil, for greasing
    and frying

3¼ cups white bread flour

4   tablespoons cold butter,
     cut into pieces

2   tablespoons sugar

½   teaspoon salt

1   package (2¼ teaspoons)
     active dry yeast

1   egg, lightly beaten

¾   cup lukewarm whole milk

Filling

½   cup seedless strawberry or
     raspberry jelly

- Lightly grease a large bowl and 2 baking sheets.

- Place the flour in a large bowl, add the butter and rub it in until the mixture resembles breadcrumbs. Stir in the sugar, salt and yeast. Make a well in the center and add the egg and milk, then mix to form a soft, pliable dough. Knead well for 10 minutes.

- Place in the greased bowl and cover. Leave in a warm place to rise for about 1 hour or until double in bulk.

- Knead the dough on a floured work surface, then divide into 10 pieces. Shape each piece into a ball, and place on the baking sheets. Cover and leave in a warm place to double in size for 45 minutes.

- Heat 3–4 inches of oil in a saucepan to 360°F, and deep–fry the donuts in batches for 2–3 minutes on each side. Drain on a paper towel, and dust with sugar.

- To fill the donuts, place the jam in a pastry bag fitted with a plain tip. Insert a sharp knife into each donut, and twist to make a hole. Push the point of the tip into the hole, and pipe in some jam.

Chocolate Cake DONUTS

Makes 10–14 donuts

Batter

½ cup whole milk (warmed)
1 egg
1 teaspoon vanilla extract
⅓ cup cocoa powder
1¾ cups all-purpose flour
½ teaspoon baking powder
½ teaspoon baking soda
½ teaspoon salt
½ cup sugar
2 tablespoons of butter
Vegetable oil for greasing baking
    sheet and frying

Glaze

¼ cup dark chocolate pieces
¼ cup white chocolate pieces

- In a bowl, blend together the warmed milk, egg and vanilla extract.

- In a mixer set up with a paddle attachment, mix the cocoa powder, flour, baking powder, baking soda, salt and sugar. Add the butter and blend. Slowly add the milk, egg and vanilla. Mix until the batter is smooth and thick and resembles cookie dough.

- Leave the dough to rest in the mixer for 20 minutes.

- Roll the dough out onto a floured surface. When the dough is ½-inch thick, use a donut cutter to cut out the donuts.

- Heat at least 3 inches of vegetable oil in a heavy bottomed pan. The oil should be 360°F. Carefully place the donuts one at a time into the oil. Fry for 2 minutes on each side or until golden brown. Remove with a slotted spoon and drain on a wire rack.

- To make the glaze, melt each of the chocolates separately over a pan of gently simmering water. Coat the donuts making a pattern.

Spiced DONUT HOLES

Makes 18–20 holes

Batter

½ cup whole milk (warm)
1 egg
2 tablespoons plain yogurt
1 teaspoon vanilla extract
1¾ cups all-purpose flour
2 teaspoons baking powder
½ teaspoon salt
⅓ cup sugar
1 teaspoon grated nutmeg
2 tablespoons butter
Vegetable oil for frying
Confectioners' sugar for dusting

- In a bowl, blend together the warm milk, egg, yogurt and vanilla extract.

- In a mixer fitted with a paddle attachment, mix the flour, baking powder, salt, sugar and nutmeg. Slowly add the butter and blend. Slowly add the milk mixture until the batter is smooth and thick and resembles cookie dough.

- Leave the dough to rest in the mixer for 20 minutes.

- Heat at least 3 inches vegetable oil in a heavy saucepan to 360°F.

- Drop dough 1 tablespoon at a time into the oil. Fry for 1 minute or until golden brown. Remove and drain on a paper towel or wire rack.

- Sprinkle with confectioners' sugar and serve.

Black & White
BROWNIES

Makes 24 brownies

Chocolate Mix

8   tablespoons (1 stick) butter

2   cups semisweet
     chocolate pieces

6   eggs

2¼ cups sugar

1½ cups all-purpose flour

1½ teaspoons baking powder

1½ teaspoons salt

1½ tablespoons vanilla extract

1   teaspoon almond extract

Cream Cheese Mix

6   tablespoons (¾ stick) butter,
     softened

1   cup cream cheese, softened

¾   cup sugar

3   eggs

3   tablespoons all-purpose flour

1   tablespoon vanilla extract

- Preheat oven to 350°F.

- Grease a 13x9–inch baking pan.

- Prepare the chocolate mix. Slowly melt the chocolate and the 8 tablespoons butter in a glass bowl placed over a pan of gently simmering water. Mix well, and set aside to cool.

- To make the cream cheese mix, cream the 6 tablespoons butter, then add the cream cheese and sugar. Beat until fluffy, and add in the eggs, then the flour and vanilla extract.

- In a separate bowl, whip the eggs and sugar until fluffy. Stir together the flour, baking powder and salt, then mix into egg mixture. Mix in the melted chocolate and butter, and add the vanilla and almond extract.

- Spread half the chocolate mixture into the pan. Then spread with the cream cheese mixture. Spoon the remaining chocolate batter on top. Swirl the two mixtures together with a knife.

- Bake for 40 minutes. Cool, and cut into bars.

Chocolate Fudge BROWNIES

Makes 9 brownies

Batter

1¼ cups semisweet chocolate pieces
8   tablespoons (1 stick) butter
1   cup sugar
Pinch of salt
2   tablespoons water
2   large eggs
1   teaspoon vanilla extract
¾   cup all-purpose flour
½   cup chopped walnuts (optional)

- Preheat oven to 325°F.

- Grease an 8-inch square baking pan.

- Place the chocolate, butter, sugar, salt and water in small saucepan over a very low flame. Heat, stirring often, until the chocolate and butter are melted and the sugar dissolved.

- Pour into a mixing bowl. Stir in the eggs, one at a time. Stir in the vanilla extract. Stir in the flour. Fold in nuts (optional). Pour the batter into the prepared pan.

- Bake for 35 minutes. Cool completely before cutting into 9 squares.

- Dust with confectioners' sugar, if desired.

Entenmann's celebrated its 100-year anniversary by commissioning replicas of its famous delivery trucks.

Double Chocolate BROWNIES

Makes 9 brownies

Batter

8	tablespoons (1 stick) butter
⅔	cup semisweet chocolate pieces
1⅓	cups sugar

Pinch of salt

1	teaspoon vanilla extract
2	eggs
1	cup all-purpose flour
2	tablespoons cocoa powder
½	cup white chocolate chips

Fudge Sauce

4	tablespoons (½ stick) butter
1	cup sugar
⅔	cup whole milk
1	cup heavy cream
⅔	cup dark corn syrup
1	cup semisweet chocolate pieces

- Preheat the oven to 350°F.

- Grease an 8-inch square cake pan, and line the bottom with parchment paper.

- Place the butter and chocolate in a small heatproof bowl set over a saucepan of gently simmering water until melted. Stir until smooth. Let cool slightly. Stir in the sugar, salt and vanilla extract. Add the eggs, one at a time, stirring well, until blended.

- Sift the flour and cocoa into the brownie batter, and beat until smooth. Stir in the white chocolate chips, then pour the batter into the prepared pan.

- Bake in the preheated oven for 35-40 minutes or until the top is evenly colored and a toothpick inserted into the center comes out almost clean. Let cool slightly while you prepare the sauce.

- To make the fudge sauce, place the butter, sugar, milk, cream and corn syrup in a small saucepan, and heat gently until the sugar has dissolved. Bring to a boil and stir for 10 minutes or until the mixture is caramel-colored. Remove from the heat, and add the chocolate. Stir until smooth. Cut the brownies into squares and serve immediately with the sauce.

Apple & Cinnamon BARS

Makes 14 bars

8   tablespoons (1 stick) unsalted
     butter, softened
⅔   cup sugar
1   teaspoon vanilla extract
2   eggs, beaten
1   cup all-purpose flour
2   large baking apples (2 cups diced)
2   tablespoons lemon juice

Topping
⅓   cup finely chopped,
     blanched almonds
¼   cup all-purpose flour
¼   cup firmly packed
     light brown sugar
½   teaspoon ground cinnamon
2   tablespoons unsalted butter,
     melted

- Preheat the oven to 350°F.

- Grease and line a 11x7-inch cake pan with parchment paper.

- Cream together the butter, sugar and vanilla extract until pale. Gradually add the eggs, beating thoroughly. Sift in the flour and fold in evenly.

- Prepare the apples by peeling, coring and dicing and sprinkling with the lemon juice. Add to the flour mixture and combine.

- Spread the mixture into the bottom of the cake pan. Pat the mixture down with the back of a wooden spoon or spatula.

- For the topping, mix all the ingredients to a crumbly texture and sprinkle over the bars. Bake the bars in the preheated oven for 45–55 minutes, until firm and golden.

- Cut into bars, and serve warm or cooled.

Lemon Drizzle BARS

Makes 12 bars

Batter
2 eggs
¾ cup sugar
12 tablespoons (1½ sticks) soft margarine
Finely grated zest of 1 lemon
1½ cups self-rising flour
½ cup whole milk

Syrup
1¼ cups confectioners' sugar
¼ cup fresh lemon juice
Confectioners' sugar, for dusting

- Preheat the oven to 350°F.

- Grease an 8-inch square cake pan, and line with parchment paper.

- Place the eggs, sugar and margarine in a bowl, and beat hard until smooth and fluffy. Stir in the lemon zest, then fold in the flour lightly and evenly. Stir in the milk, mixing evenly, then spoon the batter into the prepared cake pan, smoothing level.

- Bake in the preheated oven for 45-50 minutes or until golden brown and firm to the touch. Remove from the oven, and place the pan on a wire rack.

- To make the syrup, place the confectioners' sugar and lemon juice in a small saucepan and heat gently, stirring until the sugar dissolves. Do not boil.

- Prick the warm bars all over with a skewer, and spoon the hot syrup evenly over the top.

- Let cool completely in the pan, then remove and cut into 12 pieces. Dust with confectioners' sugar before serving.

Blueberry CRUMB CAKE

Serves 9–12

Cake Batter

2   cups all-purpose flour
1   cup sugar
2   teaspoons baking powder
¾   teaspoon baking soda
1   teaspoon salt
1½ teaspoons cinnamon
1   teaspoon nutmeg
12 tablespoons (1½ sticks) cold, unsalted butter
2   large eggs, lightly beaten
1   cup sour cream
¼   cup milk
2   teaspoons vanilla extract
2   teaspoons lemon extract
3   cups fresh blueberries

Topping

2   tablespoons sugar
3   tablespoons unsalted butter
¾   cup all-purpose flour
2   tablespoons chopped nuts (optional)

- Preheat oven to 375°F. Butter a 13x9x2-inch baking pan, and line with parchment paper.

- Whisk together flour, sugar, baking powder, baking soda, salt, cinnamon and nutmeg, and put to one side.

- Blend butter into the flour mixture with fingertips or a pastry blender until the mixture resembles a fine crumb.

- Whisk together the eggs, sour cream, milk and vanilla, and add the flour mixture, stirring until combined. Fold the blueberries and lemon extract into the batter before adding the mix to the baking pan.

- To make the crumb topping, blend the butter with the all-purpose flour until the mixture resembles crumbs. Add sugar. Stir in the chopped nuts (optional). Sprinkle over the batter mix.

- Bake until the cake is golden or when tested a toothpick comes out clean (generally 40 to 50 minutes). Cool the cake in pan for 20 minutes before serving.

Cinnamon CRUMB CAKE

Serves 9–12

Cake Batter

2½ cups all-purpose flour
1 teaspoon baking soda
¾ teaspoon baking powder
½ teaspoon salt
12 tablespoons (1½ sticks) unsalted butter
1½ cups sugar
2 large eggs
1½ cups sour cream
2 teaspoons vanilla extract

Crumb

1 cup firmly packed light brown sugar
½ cup sugar
2 teaspoons ground cinnamon
1 teaspoon ground nutmeg
½ teaspoon salt
2 sticks unsalted butter, melted
2½ cups all-purpose flour

- Preheat the oven to 350°F. Butter a 13x9x2-inch glass baking dish.

- To make the cake batter, sift the flour, baking soda, baking powder and salt into a medium bowl.

- Using an electric mixer, beat the butter in a large bowl until smooth. Add the sugar, and beat until light and fluffy. Add eggs, one at a time, beating until well blended. Add sour cream and vanilla extract, and beat until blended. Add flour mixture in 3 additions, beating until incorporated after each addition.

- Transfer half the cake batter to prepared baking dish and spread evenly with spatula.

- To make the crumb, mix both sugars, cinnamon, nutmeg and salt in medium bowl. Add warm melted butter and stir. Add flour and toss with fork until moist clumps form. Squeeze small handfuls of topping together to form small clumps. Drop the clumps evenly into the middle of the cake batter. Add the remaining cake batter to the dish, covering the crumb.

- Bake for 45–50 minutes until toothpick inserted into center comes out clean. Cool in the dish for at least 30 minutes before removing. Cut cake into squares and serve slightly warm or at room temperature.

Cream Cheese Swirl COFFEE CAKE

Serves 9–12

Cream Cheese Mix

1   cup cream cheese, softened
2   tablespoons confectioners' sugar
1½ tablespoons lemon juice

Cake Batter

2   cups all-purpose flour
1   teaspoon baking powder
1   teaspoon baking soda
1   pinch salt
1   cup sugar
8   tablespoons (1 stick) butter, softened
3   eggs, room temperature
2   teaspoons vanilla extract
1   cup sour cream

Topping

¼   cup finely chopped walnuts
2   tablespoons sugar
½   teaspoon cinnamon
½   teaspoon nutmeg

- Preheat oven to 350°F. Grease and flour a 9 x 13-inch baking pan.

- To make the cream cheese mix, in a small bowl, beat cream cheese, confectioners' sugar and lemon juice until smooth. Set aside.

- To make the cake batter, stir together flour, baking powder, baking soda and salt. Set aside.

- In a large mixer bowl, beat the sugar and butter until fluffy. Add the eggs and vanilla, mixing well. Add dry ingredients alternately with sour cream. Mix well.

- Pour half of batter into the pan. Spoon the cream cheese mixture on top of batter within ½ inch of pan edge. Spoon the remaining batter over the filling, spreading to the pan edge.

- To make the topping, combine the chopped walnuts, sugar, cinnamon and nutmeg. Sprinkle over the batter.

- Bake for 40-45 minutes or until a toothpick inserted near the center comes out clean. Cool for 10 minutes before removing from the pan. Serve warm.

By the 1950s, the Bay Shore bakery even topped Frank Sinatra's list. The American icon placed weekly orders for Entenmann's Crumb Coffee Cake.

Pumpkin
CRUMB CAKE

Serves 8–10

Cake Batter

1¾ cups all-purpose flour

1½ teaspoons pumpkin pie spice

1   teaspoon baking soda

1   teaspoon baking powder

¾   teaspoon salt

8   tablespoons (1 stick) unsalted
     butter

1¼ cups sugar

3   large eggs

1   cup canned pureed pumpkin

1   teaspoon vanilla extract

⅓   cup milk

¾   cup chopped walnuts (optional)

Topping

⅔   cup plus 2 tablespoons rolled oats

½   cup all-purpose flour

½   cup firmly packed light
     brown sugar

½   teaspoon cinnamon

6   tablespoons unsalted butter

- Preheat oven to 350°F.

- Grease a 9x5x3-inch loaf pan and line with parchment paper.

- To make the topping, combine ⅔ cup oats, flour, sugar and cinnamon in food processor. Add butter, and pulse until crumbly. Transfer mixture to medium bowl. Stir in remaining 2 tablespoons oats. Set to one side.

- Sift the flour, pumpkin spice, baking soda, baking powder and salt into a bowl.

- In a separate bowl, beat the butter with an electric mixer until smooth. Gradually beat in the sugar and 1 egg at a time.

- Add the pumpkin and vanilla extract to the wet batter mix. Gradually beat the dry ingredients into the batter. Slowly add the milk, and stir in the walnuts (optional). Transfer the batter to the prepared pan, and spread with the topping.

- Bake the loaf cake until a toothpick inserted into center comes out clean, about 55 minutes. Cool in the pan for 15 minutes.

- Transfer the cake onto a rack, and cool completely.

Apricot Crumble CAKE

Serves 9–12

Cake Batter

2 cups all-purpose flour

1 teaspoon baking powder

1 teaspoon baking soda

¾ teaspoon salt

8 tablespoons (1 stick) unsalted butter, softened

1 cup sugar

1 teaspoon vanilla extract

2 large eggs

1 cup well-shaken buttermilk

Filling

¼ cup apricot preserves for filling

Topping

2 cups flaked coconut

⅔ cup firmly packed light brown sugar

1 teaspoon cinnamon

⅓ cup melted butter

¼ cup apricot preserves

- Preheat the oven to 350°F.

- Line the bottom of a 9x2-inch round cake pan with parchment paper, and butter the paper.

- To make the cake batter, sift together the flour, baking powder, baking soda and salt.

- Beat together the butter and sugar in a large bowl with an electric mixer until pale and fluffy, then beat in the vanilla extract. Add eggs one at a time, beating well after each addition, then, with mixer at low speed, beat in all of the buttermilk until just combined. Add flour mixture in 3 batches, mixing after each addition until just combined.

- Spoon batter into the cake pan, and bake for 45–50 minutes until golden and a toothpick inserted in the middle comes out clean.

- Cool in the pan for 10 minutes before removing. Invert onto rack, then slide cake onto a baking sheet and heat broiler to high. Slice the cake in half horizontally, and spread the apricot preserves on the bottom half, then place the other half on top.

- For the topping, combine the coconut, brown sugar, cinnamon-melted butter and apricot preserves. Mix well. Spread onto the top of the cake, and broil for 3-5 minutes until golden brown.

Blueberry Sour Cream LOAF CAKE

Serves 8–10

Batter

3¼ cups all-purpose flour
1   teaspoon salt
24 tablespoons (3 sticks) unsalted
    butter
½   cup sour cream
2   cups sugar
1½ teaspoons vanilla extract
8   large eggs
2   cups blueberries
2   tablespoons all-purpose flour
¼   cup sugar for sprinkling
    onto prepared batter

Glaze

1   cup heavy cream
1   tablespoon confectioners' sugar
2   teaspoons lemon zest

- Preheat the oven to 350°F.

- Grease two 9x5x3-inch loaf pans, and line with parchment paper.

- Combine the flour and salt in a bowl and set aside.

- With an electric mixer, cream butter, sour cream and sugar on high speed until pale and fluffy. Add the vanilla extract.

- Lightly beat 8 eggs and add to the creamed butter mixture. Toss blueberries in 2 tablespoons of the flour. Mix remaining flour and salt into the batter, then fold in blueberries.

- Divide the batter between the pans. Sprinkle 2 tablespoons of sugar over each cake.

- Bake until a toothpick inserted into center of each cake comes out clean, about 65 minutes.

- Cool on a wire rack for 30 minutes before removing the cakes from the pans.

- To make the glaze, mix together the cream, sugar and lemon zest. Spread on the cake or serve on the side.

Lemon LOAF CAKE

Serves 8–10

Batter

1½ cups all-purpose flour

1 tablespoon baking powder

12 tablespoons (1½ sticks) butter, softened

¾ cup sugar

3 eggs, beaten

1 egg yolk

Finely grated zest of 1 lemon

2 tablespoons lemon juice

Fine strips of lemon zest, to decorate

Syrup

¾ cup confectioners' sugar

3 tablespoons lemon juice

- Preheat the oven to 350°F.

- Grease a 9x5x3-inch loaf pan, and line with parchment paper.

- Sift the flour and baking powder into a large bowl, and add the butter, sugar, eggs and egg yolk. Beat well until the mixture is smooth, then stir in the lemon zest and juice.

- Spoon the mixture into the prepared pan and smooth the surface with a spatula. Bake in the preheated oven for 40–50 minutes, or until well risen and golden brown. Remove the pan from the oven, and transfer to a wire rack.

- For the syrup, put the confectioners' sugar and lemon juice into a pan, and heat gently without boiling, stirring until the sugar dissolves.

- Prick the top of the loaf several times with a toothpick, and spoon the syrup over it. Let cool completely in the pan, then take out, sprinkle with strips of lemon zest and serve in slices.

In 1951, the Entenmann family, Martha and her sons Charles, Robert and William, took over the management of Entenmann's and brought the brand into supermarkets.

Orange Glaze
LOAF CAKE

Serves 8–10

Batter

2   cups all-purpose flour
1   teaspoon baking powder
¼   teaspoon baking soda
½   teaspoon salt
16 tablespoons (2 sticks) unsalted butter
1¼ cups sugar
1   tablespoon grated lemon zest
1   tablespoon grated orange zest
4   eggs
1   teaspoon vanilla extract
½   cup buttermilk

Glaze

1   cup confectioners' sugar
1½ tablespoons fresh orange juice
1   tablespoon freshly grated orange zest

- Preheat oven to 325°F.

- Grease a 9x5x3-inch loaf pan, and line with parchment paper.

- Sift together the flour, baking powder, baking soda and salt in a mixing bowl.

- In a large mixing bowl, using an electric mixer, beat the butter, sugar and zests until light and creamy. Beat in the eggs, one at a time, beating very thoroughly after each addition. Add the vanilla extract.

- Using a spatula, mix in the flour alternately with the buttermilk, ending with flour.

- Scrape the batter into the prepared loaf pan.

- Bake for 60 minutes or until a toothpick inserted in the center comes out clean. Remove and let rest for 15 minutes, then turn onto a cooling rack. Let cool for 15 more minutes before glazing.

- To make the glaze: In a bowl, combine the sugar and orange zest, adding enough orange juice to get a smooth spreadable consistency. Apply to the top of the warm cake. Let the loaf cake cool completely before serving.

Chocolate Chip Coffee
LOAF CAKE

Serves 8–10

Batter

3¼ cups all-purpose flour

1 teaspoon salt

32 tablespoons (4 sticks) unsalted butter

2 cups sugar

1½ teaspoons vanilla extract

8 large eggs, lightly beaten

2 cups semisweet chocolate chips

Glaze

1 cup semisweet chocolate chips

5 tablespoons coffee liqueur

1 tablespoon vanilla extract

1 tablespoon light corn syrup

- Preheat the oven to 350°F.

- Grease two 9x5x3-inch loaf pans, and line with parchment paper.

- Combine the flour and salt in a bowl, and set aside.

- With an electric mixer, cream the butter and sugar until pale and fluffy. Stir in the vanilla extract.

- In a large bowl, lightly beat the 8 eggs, and add to the butter and sugar mix. Fold in the flour, and mix thoroughly. Fold the semisweet chocolate chips into the finished batter. Divide the batter between the pans.

- Bake until a toothpick inserted into center of each cake comes out clean, about 65 minutes. Let cool in pans on a wire rack for 30 minutes before removing from the pans.

- To make glaze, heat the chocolate chips, coffee liquer, vanilla extract and light corn syrup in a glass bowl set in a simmering pan of water. Whisk until smooth.

- Pour over cake, and for a special treat, serve with whipped cream.

Marble Loaf CAKE

Serves 8–10

Batter

⅓ cup semisweet chocolate pieces
3 tablespoons whole milk
5 tablespoons butter
½ cup sugar
1 egg, beaten
3 tablespoons sour cream
1 cup self-rising flour
½ teaspoon baking powder
½ teaspoon vanilla extract

- Preheat the oven to 325°F.

- Grease a 9x5x3-inch loaf pan, and line with parchment paper.

- Combine chocolate and milk in a small heatproof bowl, and set the bowl over a saucepan of simmering water.

- Cream together the butter and sugar until light and fluffy. Beat in the egg and sour cream. Sift the flour and baking powder over the mixture, then fold in using a rubber spatula.

- Spoon half the batter into a separate bowl, and stir in the chocolate mixture.

- Add the vanilla extract to the plain batter.

- Spoon the chocolate and vanilla batters alternately into the prepared loaf pan, swirling lightly with a knife for a marbled effect. Bake for 40–45 minutes or until well risen and a toothpick when inserted comes out clean.

- Cool in the pan for 10 minutes, then turn out and finish cooling on a wire rack.

Chocolate *Peanut Butter* LOAF CAKE

Serves 8–10

Batter

2¼ cups all-purpose flour
1 cup unsweetened cocoa powder
1 teaspoon salt
32 tablespoons (4 sticks) unsalted butter
2 cups sugar
1½ teaspoons vanilla extract
8 large eggs
2 cups semisweet chocolate chips

Glaze

¼ cup peanut butter
5 tablespoons whole milk

- Preheat oven to 350°F.

- Grease two 9x5x3-inch loaf pans, and line with parchment paper.

- Combine the flour, cocoa powder and salt in a bowl, and set aside.

- Cream the butter and sugar with an electric mixer on high speed until pale and fluffy. Add the vanilla extract.

- Lightly beat 8 eggs, and add to the butter and sugar mix, mixing until just incorporated. Add the flour mixture, and beat until just combined. Fold in the chocolate chips.

- Divide the batter between the pans. Bake until a toothpick inserted into center of each cake comes out clean, about 65 minutes.

- Cool in pans on a wire rack for 30 minutes before removing.

- To make the glaze, combine the peanut butter and milk and whisk until smooth. Add more milk, if necessary, to achieve the desired consistency. Spread over the cooled loaf.

In the 1950s, the family expanded the business into New Jersey and Connecticut. In 1961, Entenmann's built the largest baking facility of its kind in the U.S. on five acres in Bay Shore, Long Island.

Fresh Blueberry PIE

Serves 8

Pie Crust

2 cups all-purpose flour
½ teaspoon salt
1 cup cold vegetable shortening,
   cut into small pieces
¼ cup whole milk
2 tablespoons vinegar

Filling

¾ cup sugar
3 tablespoons cornstarch
¼ teaspoon salt
½ teaspoon ground cinnamon
½ teaspoon ground nutmeg
4 cups fresh blueberries
1 tablespoon butter

- Preheat oven to 425°F. Lightly grease a 9-inch pie pan or line with parchment paper.

- Sift the flour and salt into a bowl, and cut in the shortening with a pastry blender or your fingertips until it is the size of small peas.

- Combine the milk and vinegar in a separate bowl. Using a fork add the milk mixture 1 tablespoon at a time until the dry ingredients are lightly moistened and holding together.

- Divide the dough in half, and roll out one half on a lightly floured surface to a circle about 12 inches in diameter. Line the pie pan.

- Bake the bottom crust on lower shelf of the oven for about 15 minutes or until crust is golden brown.

- To make the filling, mix the sugar, cornstarch, salt, cinnamon and nutmeg, and sprinkle over the blueberries.

- Cut the remaining pie crust into ½– ¾ –inch wide strips, and make a lattice top. Crimp and flute the edges.

- Bake the pie on the lower shelf of the oven for about 50 minutes or until the crust is golden brown. Serve warm or cooled.

Cherry PIE

Serves 8

Pie Crust

1 cup all-purpose flour

¼ teaspoon baking powder

½ teaspoon allspice

½ teaspoon salt

¼ cup sugar

4 tablespoons cold unsalted butter, cut into small pieces

1 egg, beaten, plus extra for glazing

Filling

4 cups (2 lbs) pitted fresh cherries or drained canned cherries

½ cup sugar

½ teaspoon almond extract

2 teaspoons cherry brandy

¼ teaspoon allspice

2 tablespoons cornstarch

2 tablespoons water

2 tablespoons unsalted butter

- Preheat the oven to 425°F. Grease a 9-inch round tart pan.

- To make the pie crusts, sift the flour and baking powder into a large bowl. Stir in the allspice, salt and sugar. Rub in the butter with your fingertips until the mixture resembles fine breadcrumbs. Add the beaten egg, and mix to a firm dough. Cut the dough in half, and roll each half into a ball. Roll out one half of the dough, and line the pan.

- To make the filling, put half of the cherries and the sugar in a large saucepan. Bring to a simmer over low heat, stirring, until the sugar has dissolved. Stir in the almond extract, brandy and allspice. In a separate bowl, mix the cornstarch and water to form a paste. Remove the saucepan from the heat, stir in the cornstarch paste, then return to the heat and stir continuously until the mixture boils. Stir in the remaining cherries. Pour into the pastry shell.

- Cut the remaining dough into long strips about ½-inch wide. Lay 5 strips evenly across the top of the filling. Now lay 6 strips crosswise over the strips, folding back every other strip each time you add another crosswise strip to form a lattice. Trim off the ends and seal the edges with water. Use your fingers to crimp around the rim, then brush the top with beaten egg to glaze. Cover with foil and bake for 30 minutes. Discard the foil, then bake for an additional 15 minutes or until the crust is golden.

Simple Apple PIE

Serves 8

Pie Crust

2 ready-made pie crusts,
 thaw if frozen

1 beaten egg to glaze the pastry

Filling

6 baking apples (6 cups peeled
 and sliced)

⅓ cup lemon juice

1 cup sugar

3 tablespoons cornstarch

Pinch of nutmeg

½ teaspoon cinnamon

2 tablespoons butter

- Preheat oven to 375°F. Grease a 9-inch pie pan.

- Roll 1 dough on a lightly floured surface to form the bottom crust. It should be rolled large enough to cover the pan with a few inches to spare all around. Place and press into the pan.

- For the filling, peel, core and slice the apples into thin slices. Toss the apple slices with the lemon juice in a large mixing bowl. Add the rest of the filling ingredients, except the butter, and mix until well combined.

- Pour the apple mixture into the bottom crust. Dot the top of the apples with the butter.

- Roll out the second pie crust and cover the mounded apples. Press the two pieces of dough together with your fingers. Pinch the edges so that both crusts are sealed all the way around the pan.

- Cut a few slashes in the top crust so the steam can escape. Brush the top crust with the beaten egg. Bake for 1–1½ hours, until the crust is nicely browned, and the apples are tender when tested with a small knife through the slits on the top. If the crust begins to brown too quickly, tent with foil.

- Serve warm or cooled.

Chocolate Pumpkin PIE

Serves 8

Pie Crust

2 cups finely ground graham crackers

6 tablespoons butter, melted

1 tablespoon sugar

2 tablespoons firmly packed light brown sugar

½ teaspoon salt

½ teaspoon ground cinnamon

¼ cup bittersweet chocolate, chopped

Filling

¾ cup semisweet chocolate, pieces

4 tablespoons unsalted butter

1 (15-ounce) can pumpkin purée

1 (12-ounce) can evaporated milk

¾ cup firmly packed light brown sugar

3 large eggs

1 tablespoon cornstarch

2 teaspoons vanilla extract

1½ teaspoons salt

2 teaspoons pumpkin pie spice

- Preheat oven to 350°F and grease a 9-inch pie pan.

- To make the crust, combine the graham cracker crumbs, butter, sugars, salt and cinnamon in a bowl. Firmly press the mixture into the bottom and up the sides of the pie pan. Bake until firm, 8 to 10 minutes.

- Remove from the oven, and sprinkle the bittersweet chocolate over bottom of crust. Return to the oven to melt the chocolate, about 1 minute. Spread the chocolate in a thin layer on the bottom and up the sides. Let cool on a wire rack and reduce the oven temperature to 325°F degrees.

- To make the filling, in a large heatproof bowl, set over a pot of simmering water. Melt the semisweet chocolate and butter, stirring until smooth. Remove from the heat.

- Mix the pumpkin purée, milk, brown sugar, eggs, cornstarch, vanilla, salt and pumpkin pie spice in a medium bowl. Whisk ⅓ pumpkin mixture into chocolate mixture. Whisk in remaining pumpkin mixture.

- Transfer the pie pan to a rimmed baking sheet, and pour the pumpkin mixture into crust. Bake until the center is set, but still a bit wobbly, 55-60 minutes. Let cool in pie dish on a wire rack. Refrigerate until well chilled, at least 8 hours.

Candied Sweet Potato PIE

Serves 8

Pie Crust

1¼ cups all-purpose flour

½ teaspoon salt

¼ teaspoon sugar

1½ tablespoons cold butter, diced

3 tablespoons vegetable shortening

2–2½ tablespoons ice-cold water

Filling

2 cups mashed cooked sweet potatoes

3 extra-large eggs, beaten

½ cup firmly packed dark brown sugar

1½ cups evaporated milk

3 tablespoons butter, melted

2 teaspoons vanilla extract

1 teaspoon ground cinnamon

1 teaspoon ground nutmeg

½ teaspoon salt

Freshly whipped cream, to serve

- Preheat oven to 425°F. Grease a 9-inch pie pan.

- To make the pie crust, sift the flour, salt and sugar into a bowl. Add the butter and vegetable shortening to the bowl, and rub in with the fingertips until fine crumbs form. Sprinkle over 2 tablespoons of the water, and mix with a fork until a soft dough forms. Wrap in plastic wrap, and chill for at least 1 hour.

- To make the filling, put the sweet potatoes in a separate bowl and beat in the eggs and sugar until very smooth. Beat in the remaining ingredients, except the whipped cream, then set aside.

- Roll out the dough on a lightly floured surface into a thin 11-inch circle, and line the pie pan. Trim off the excess dough. Prick the base of the pastry shell all over with the fork, and place crumpled kitchen foil in the center. Bake for 12 minutes or until golden.

- Remove the pie shell from the oven, take out the foil, pour the filling into the shell and return to the oven for an additional 10 minutes. Reduce the oven temperature to 325°F, and bake for an additional 35 minutes or until a knife inserted into the center comes out clean. Let cool on a cooling rack. Serve warm or at room temperature with whipped cream.

Gingerbread and Vanilla WHOOPIE PIES

Makes 14

1 egg
⅓ cup light brown sugar
1 tablespoon molasses
3 tablespoons unsalted butter, melted
5 tablespoons milk
1 cup all-purpose flour
½ teaspoon baking soda
1½ teaspoons ground ginger
½ teaspoon ground allspice

Filling

½ cup cream cheese
1 tablespoon unsalted butter, softened
1 teaspoon vanilla extract
1 cup confectioners' sugar
1 teaspoon boiling water

- Preheat the oven to 350°F. Line 2 baking sheets with parchment paper.

- Put the egg, light brown sugar, and molasses in a mixing bowl and beat together with an electric mixer until thickened and foamy. Beat in the butter and milk.

- Sift the flour, baking soda, ginger and allspice into the bowl and stir with a wooden spoon to make a soft dough.

- Spoon teaspoons of the mixture onto the baking sheets, flattening them slightly so each spoonful is about 1 inch in diameter. Space the spoonfuls about 2 inches apart to allow for expansion.

- Bake in the preheated oven for 10 minutes or until risen and firm to the touch, rotating the baking sheets halfway through baking. Let stand on the sheets for 5 minutes, then transfer to a wire rack to cool.

- For the filling, put the cream cheese, unsalted butter, vanilla and confectioners' sugar in a mixing bowl, and beat together with an electric mixer until smooth and creamy. Beat in the boiling water to soften. Sandwich the whoopie pies together in pairs with the filling. Let stand in a cool place to firm up for a couple of hours.

A graduating class from the Entenmann's School of Baking

Chocolate WHOOPIE PIES

Makes 10

1¼ cups all-purpose flour
1½ teaspoons baking soda
½ cup cocoa powder
large pinch of salt
6 tablespoons butter, softened
⅓ cup vegetable shortening
¾ cup dark brown sugar
1 large egg, beaten
1 teaspoon vanilla extract
⅔ cup milk

Marshmallow Filling
8 ounces marshmallows
¼ cup milk
½ cup vegetable shortening
½ cup confectioners' sugar, sifted

- Preheat the oven to 350°F. Line 2-3 large baking sheets with parchment paper. Sift together the all-purpose flour, baking soda, unsweetened cocoa and salt.

- Place the butter, vegetable shortening and brown sugar in a large bowl and beat with an electric mixer until pale and fluffy. Beat in the egg and vanilla extract followed by half of the flour mixture and then the milk. Stir in the rest of the flour mixture, and mix until thoroughly incorporated.

- Pipe or spoon 20 mounds of the batter onto the prepared baking sheets, spaced well apart to allow for spreading. Bake in the preheated oven, one sheet at a time, for 12-14 minutes until risen and just firm to the touch. Cool for 5 minutes, then using a spatula, transfer to a cooling rack, and let cool completely.

- For the filling, place the marshmallows and milk in a heatproof bowl set over a pan of simmering water. Heat until the marshmallows have melted, stirring occasionally. Remove from the heat and let cool.

- Place the vegetable shortening and confectioners' sugar in a bowl and beat together until smooth and creamy. Add the creamed mixture to the marshmallow, and beat for 1-2 minutes until fluffy.

- To assemble, spread the filling over the flat side of half the cakes. Top with the remaining cakes.

Coffee WHOOPIE PIES

Makes 15

Filling

1¾ cups all-purpose flour
1   teaspoon baking soda
large pinch of salt
2   teaspoons ground cinnamon
8   tablespoons (1 stick) butter,
    softened
¾   cup superfine sugar
2   tablespoons superfine
    sugar
1   large egg, beaten
1   teaspoon vanilla extract
⅔   cup buttermilk

Coffee Filling

8   tablespoons (1 stick) unsalted
    butter, softened
½   cup cream cheese, softened
1   tablespoon strong cold
    black coffee
2½ cups confectioners' sugar, sifted

- Preheat the oven to 350°F. Line 2-3 large baking sheets with parchment paper. Sift together the all-purpose flour, baking soda, salt and 1 teaspoon of cinnamon.

- Place the butter and the ¾ cup superfine sugar in a large bowl, and beat with an electric mixer until pale and fluffy. Beat in the egg and vanilla extract followed by half of the flour mixture and then the buttermilk. Stir in the rest of the flour mixture, and mix until thoroughly incorporated.

- Pipe or spoon 30 mounds of the batter onto the prepared cookie sheets, spaced well apart to allow for spreading. Mix together the rest of the cinnamon with the 2 tablespoons of superfine sugar, and sprinkle liberally over the mounds. Bake in the preheated oven, one sheet at a time, for 10-12 minutes until risen and just firm to the touch. Cool for 5 minutes, then using a spatula, transfer to a cooling rack, and let cool completely.

- For the filling, place the butter, cream cheese and coffee in a bowl, and beat together until well blended. Gradually beat in the confectioners' sugar until smooth.

- To assemble, spread or pipe the coffee filling on the flat side of half of the cakes. Top with the rest of the cakes.

Peanut Butter & Jelly WHOOPIE PIES

Makes 14

1¾ cups all-purpose flour

1 teaspoon baking soda

large pinch of salt

8 tablespoons (1 stick) butter, softened

¾ cup light brown sugar

1 large egg, beaten

⅔ cup buttermilk

½ cup unsalted peanuts, finely ground

1 tablespoon roughly chopped salted peanuts

3 tablespoons grape jelly

Filling

8 tablespoons (1 stick) unsalted butter, softened

½ cup chunky peanut butter

1¼ cups confectioners' sugar, sifted

- Preheat the oven to 350°F. Line 2–3 large baking sheets with parchment paper. Sift together the all-purpose flour, baking soda and salt.

- Place the butter and sugar in a large bowl, and beat with an electric mixer until pale and fluffy. Beat in the egg, followed by half of the flour mixture, and then the buttermilk. Stir in the rest of the flour mixture, and mix until thoroughly incorporated. Fold in the ground peanuts.

- Pipe or spoon 28 mounds of the mixture onto the prepared baking sheets, spaced well apart to allow for spreading. Sprinkle with the chopped salted nuts. Bake, one sheet at a time, in the preheated oven for 10–12 minutes until risen and just firm to the touch. Cool for 5 minutes, then using a spatula transfer to a cooling rack, and let cool completely.

- For the filling, place the butter and peanut butter in a bowl, and beat with an electric mixer for 5 minutes until pale and fluffy. Gradually beat in the confectioners' sugar until smooth.

- To assemble, spread the filling on the flat side of half of the cakes, and top with a thin layer of jelly. Top with the rest of the cakes.

Red Velvet
WHOOPIE PIES

Makes 10

1½ cups all-purpose flour
1½ teaspoon baking soda
¼ cup cocoa powder
large pinch of salt
6 tablespoons butter, softened
⅓ cup vegetable shortening
¾ cup light brown sugar
1 large egg, beaten
1 teaspoon vanilla extract
1 tablespoon red food coloring
⅔ cup sour cream

Vanilla Filling
1 cup cream cheese, at
   room temperature
4 tablespoons unsalted butter,
   softened
few drops vanilla extract
¾ cup confectioners' sugar, sifted

- Preheat the oven to 350°F. Line 2-3 large baking sheets with parchment paper. Sift together the all-purpose flour, baking soda, unsweetened cocoa and salt.

- Place the butter, vegetable shortening and brown sugar in a large bowl, and beat with an electric mixer until pale and fluffy. Beat in the egg, vanilla extract and food coloring followed by half of the flour mixture and then the sour cream. Stir in the rest of the flour mixture, and mix until thoroughly incorporated.

- Pipe or spoon 20 mounds of the batter onto the prepared baking sheets, spaced well apart to allow for spreading. Bake, one sheet at a time, in the preheated oven for 12-14 minutes until risen and just firm to the touch. Cool for 5 minutes, then using a spatula, transfer to a cooling rack and let cool completely.

- For the filling, place the cream cheese and butter in a bowl and beat together until well blended. Beat in the vanilla extract and confectioners' sugar until smooth.

- To assemble, spread or pipe the filling over the flat side of half the cakes. Top with the rest of the cakes.

Chocolate Mint
POPS

Makes 26–28 Pops

10 ounces semisweet chocolate,
    coarsely chopped
2   tablespoon unsalted butter,
    softened
1   ounce hard mint candies
1   pound milk chocolate
1   cup coarsely chopped mini
    marshmallows
26–28 x 2-inch lollipop sticks
chocolate sprinkles, to decorate

• Line a baking sheet with parchment paper. Put the semisweet chocolate in a heatproof bowl, set the bowl over a saucepan of gently simmering water, and heat until melted. Stir in the butter. Let stand until the mixture is cool, but not beginning to set.

• Put the mint candies in a plastic bag, and tap firmly with a rolling pin until they are broken into tiny pieces. Finely chop 5 ounces of the milk chocolate, then stir it into the melted semisweet chocolate with the mints and marshmallows until thoroughly mixed.

• As soon as the mixture is firm enough to hold its shape, divide and roll into 26–28 even balls. Place the balls on the baking sheet and chill in the refrigerator for 30–60 minutes, until firm but not brittle. Push a lollipop stick into each pop, then chill for an additional 10 minutes.

• Coarsely chop the remaining milk chocolate and melt as above, then remove from the heat. Dip a pop into the chocolate, turning it until coated. Lift it from the bowl, letting the excess drip back into the bowl, and place it in a cup or glass. Sprinkle with the chocolate sprinkles. Repeat with the remaining pops. Chill or let stand in a cool place until the chocolate has set.

Mini cake POPS

Makes 24

1   Entenmann's All Butter
    Loaf Cake
3   ounces mascarpone cheese
1   cup confectioners' sugar
½   teaspoon vanilla or almond
    extract

DECORATION
8   ounces milk chocolate, coarsely
    chopped
24 lollipop sticks
1   cup confectioners' sugar
pink food coloring
4   teaspoons cold water
24   small candies, such as miniature
sugar-coated chocolate candies
sugar sprinkles

• Line a baking sheet with parchment paper. Crumble the yellow cake into a mixing bowl. Add the mascarpone, confectioners' sugar and vanilla, and mix together until you have a thick mixture.

• Divide the mixture into 24 even pieces. Roll 1 piece of the mixture into a ball. Push this ball into a mini paper liner, pressing it down so that when it is removed from the liner you have a mini cupcake shape. Shape the remaining 23 cake pops in the same way. Place on the baking sheet and chill for 1–2 hours to firm up.

• Put the chocolate in a heatproof bowl, set the bowl over a saucepan of gently simmering water, and heat until melted. Remove from the heat. Push a lollipop stick into each cake pop. Dip a cake pop into the chocolate, turning it until coated. Lift it from the bowl, letting the excess drip back into the bowl, then place it in a cup or glass. Repeat with the remaining cake pops. Chill or let stand in a cool place until the chocolate has set.

• Put the confectioners' sugar in a mixing bowl, and beat in a dash of pink food coloring and the water until smooth. The icing should almost hold its shape. Spoon a little onto a cake pop, easing it slightly down the sides with the side of a teaspoon. If the icing is too firm, you might need to add a dash more water. Before the icing sets, place a small candy in the center of each cake pop, and scatter with sugar sprinkles.

gift tags for your sweet treats...